T0029030

MARKUS MOTUM

DUCKS OVERBOARD!

A True Story of Plastic in Our Oceans

CANDLEWICK PRESS

Hello.

You may have seen plastic ducks like me before, but I'll bet none of them has had a story like mine. I've been on quite an adventure. This is the story of that incredible journey—where I came from, how I got lost, the strange and amazing sights I saw, and how I ended up here.

Where is here?
Well, first things first.

My story began in 1992 in a factory in China.

The factory molded plastic bath toys in the shape of ducks, frogs, turtles, and beavers.

Many toys are made from plastic because it is long-lasting and easy to clean.

Thousands of us ducks
were packed up in boxes.

Plastic can be an extremely useful
material and is used widely in medicine,
technology, and food storage.

Our boxes were loaded
into a container and carried
away by a large truck.

More plastic has been produced since 2004
than during the whole of the twentieth century.

Our container, along with hundreds of others, was loaded onto a ship destined for the United States, about 6,000 miles (9,600 kilometers) across the Pacific Ocean. From there, we would land in all sorts of shops and bathtubs.

At least that was the plan. Far out at sea,
the ship was caught in a fierce storm.
A giant wave swept our container
overboard, and it began to sink.

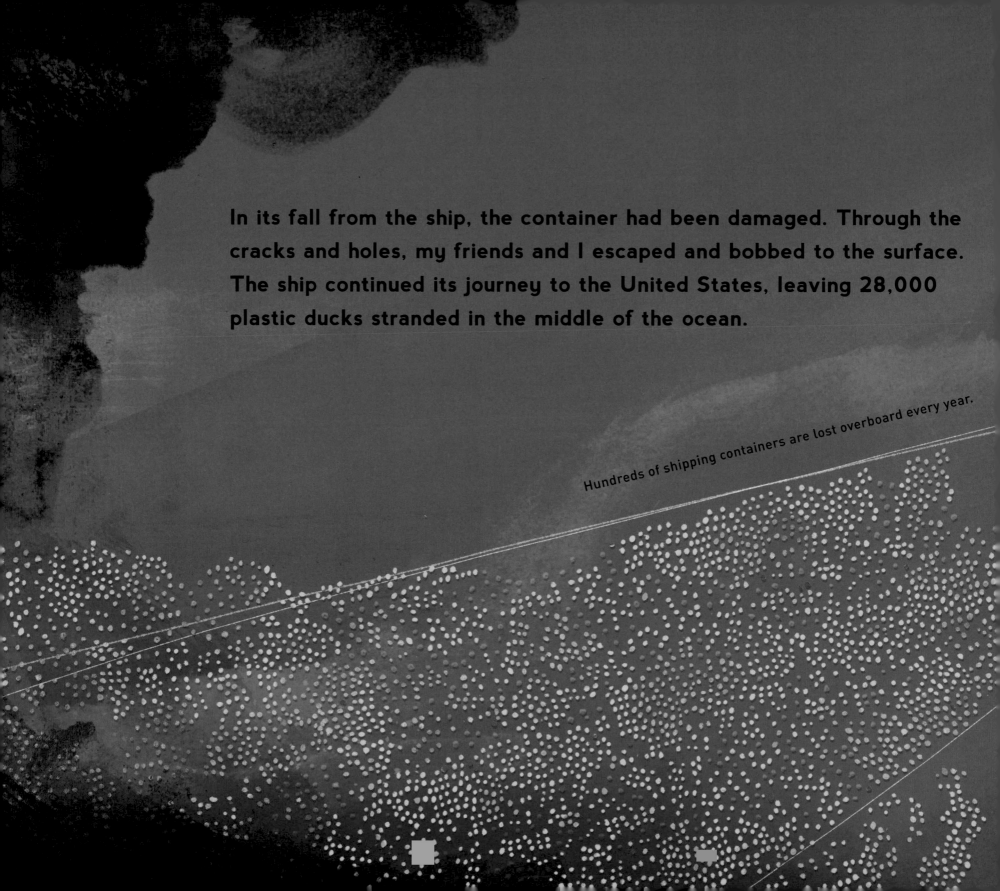

In its fall from the ship, the container had been damaged. Through the cracks and holes, my friends and I escaped and bobbed to the surface. The ship continued its journey to the United States, leaving 28,000 plastic ducks stranded in the middle of the ocean.

Hundreds of shipping containers are lost overboard every year.

Cargo floating on the sea or washed up on shore is known as flotsam. Most flotsam is never recovered.

We were buffeted by the waves, blown by the wind, and pulled by the ocean currents. We were soon separated and spread out in different directions.

A current is a steady movement of water in a particular direction. Ocean currents are driven by tides, wind, and water temperature and density.

We were surrounded by the blue ocean and the life in it.

We saw fish of every size, shape, and color. We saw a giant jellyfish and many other creatures. And we spotted something completely out of place in the ocean—

a plastic bag.

Plastic bags are "single-use" plastic, which means they are used for a very short time before being thrown away.

Before we knew it, a passing
whale gobbled it up.

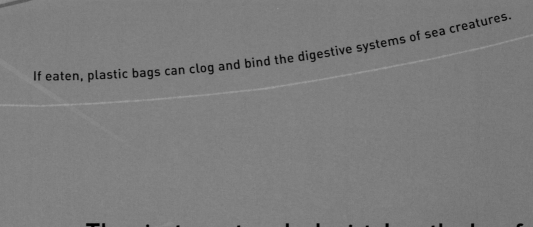

If eaten, plastic bags can clog and bind the digestive systems of sea creatures.

The giant creature had mistaken the bag for food. It swam off, still hungry, to catch up with its pod.

We carried on with our journey.

The days passed and I found myself alone, pulled by a current away from the last of my fellow travelers. One day I spotted a sea turtle struggling in the water.

Sea creatures can and do get tangled in fishing nets. The nets can make it more difficult for the animals to swim, hunt for food, or even breathe.

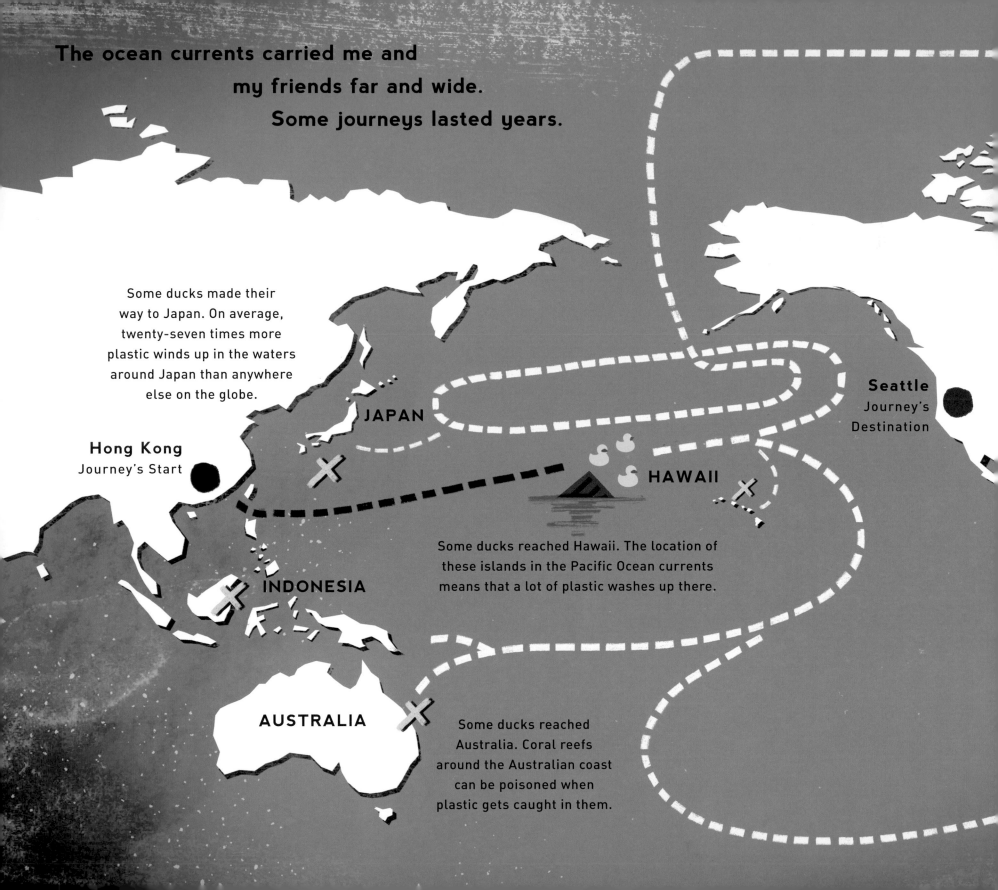

The ocean currents carried me and
my friends far and wide.
Some journeys lasted years.

Some ducks made their way to Japan. On average, twenty-seven times more plastic winds up in the waters around Japan than anywhere else on the globe.

Seattle
Journey's Destination

Hong Kong
Journey's Start

JAPAN

HAWAII

Some ducks reached Hawaii. The location of these islands in the Pacific Ocean currents means that a lot of plastic washes up there.

INDONESIA

AUSTRALIA

Some ducks reached Australia. Coral reefs around the Australian coast can be poisoned when plastic gets caught in them.

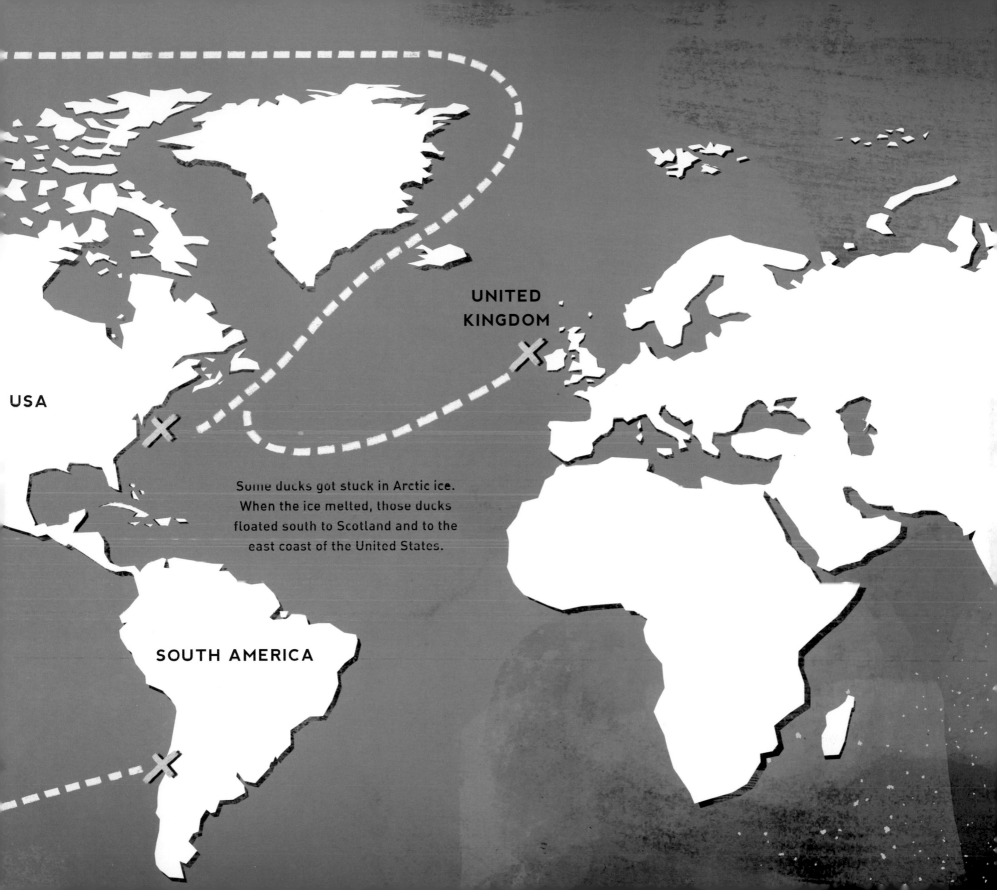

UNITED
KINGDOM

USA

Some ducks got stuck in Arctic ice.
When the ice melted, those ducks
floated south to Scotland and to the
east coast of the United States.

SOUTH AMERICA

The Great Pacific Garbage Patch is a vast area with a high concentration of marine trash.

I wasn't so lucky. The currents took me straight into a giant garbage patch!
For miles all I could see was trash: toothbrushes, bottles, cups, shoes, and more.

It is created by swirling currents that carry debris to the area and trap it. It is estimated to be more than double the size of Texas.

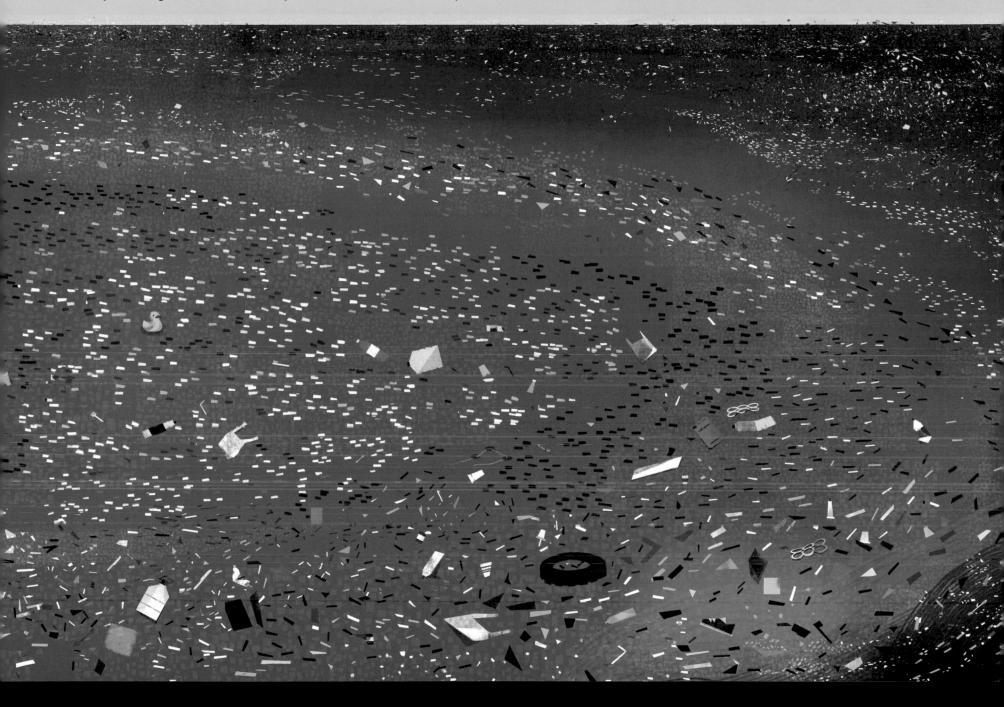

I was caught in a swirling, floating mass of trash. Was this where I belonged?

I thought I'd be stuck there forever,
part of an island of unwanted,
discarded, and forgotten things.

Then one day, clouds darkened
the sky. The wind kicked up.
The water grew wild. A mighty
storm freed me from the
garbage patch.

Across weeks,

months, and years,

the ocean
tossed me.

I floated for thousands of miles, until one day I finally reached land. Though I had never seen or been to this place before, it felt familiar. Why?

The beach was covered in trash, the same kind of trash I'd seen in oceans all over the world. Plastic, it seemed, was everywhere.

At least here, the trash was not being ignored. Up and down the beach, it was being collected, then sorted. Some of it would be recycled, while some would be cleaned, fixed, or restored to be made useful again.

Even *I* was scooped up and put in a bag. Where would I end up? I wondered.

And it was here!

LOST AT SEA

Hundreds of shipping containers are lost at sea every year. One container that spilled into the Pacific Ocean in January 1992 was filled with plastic ducks, frogs, turtles, and beavers. Scientists like Curtis Ebbesmeyer tracked the journeys of these toys, asking beachcombers to report any they found. The routes of this flotsam revealed the worldwide network of ocean currents.

Most of the plastic toys from that container have since been found all over the globe, but it's believed that about two thousand are still at large, possibly trapped by currents or even ice. Who knows where or if they will ever be seen again?

OCEAN CURRENTS

The water in our oceans is constantly on the move. We call these movements ocean currents. Tides, wind, and water temperatures and salinity affect the direction and speed of ocean currents. Currents move heat, sea creatures, and flotsam (including plastic ducks) around the oceans.

When rotating currents meet, they can create a massive whirlpool called a gyre. Floating plastic can accumulate in a gyre, where it swirls around in a big soup. There are at least five giant ocean garbage patches: one each in the North Atlantic, South Atlantic, North Pacific, South Pacific, and Indian Oceans. There may be more.

PLASTIC FACTS

✺ Much plastic can be reused or recycled. However, 40 percent of plastic produced is single-use, and is used for only a few minutes. And most single-use plastic either can't be recycled or isn't.

✺ Every year, 8.8 million tons (8 million metric tons) of plastic trash end up in the world's oceans.

✺ Plastic never disappears. It only breaks down into smaller and smaller pieces known as microplastics until you can't see it. These microplastics are harmful to sea creatures that eat them.

✺ Scientists predict that by 2050, there will be more plastic (by mass) than fish in the ocean.

HOW YOU CAN HELP

✺ A beach cleanup is a great way to keep plastic and other trash from reaching our oceans. To find out about volunteering for a beach cleanup near you, check out www.oceanconservancy.org or www.blueoceansociety.org. Who knows? You might even find a lost yellow duck!

✺ If you don't live near the sea, there are still ways you can help keep plastic out of the ocean. Always recycle what you can, and put your garbage in trash receptacles—this helps keep plastic out of lakes, and out of streams and rivers, which lead to the ocean.

✺ Many people have been working together to fight plastic pollution, and some campaigns and organizations have been started by kids or young adults. Amy and Ella Meek started Kids Against Plastic in the UK. Young adult Kristal Ambrose launched the nonprofit Bahamas Plastic Movement. Sisters Melati and Isabel Witsjen persuaded the governor of the Indonesian island of Bali to ban the use of plastic bags and straws. And teenager Hannah Testa successfully lobbied her home state of Georgia to create a Plastic Pollution Awareness Day.

✺ Make your voice heard, too, by signing petitions against single-use plastics and by urging local, state, and federal officials to take action.

For Isabella and Adriana

Copyright © 2021 by Markus Motum

All rights reserved. No part of this book may be reproduced, transmitted, or stored in an information retrieval system in any form or by any means, graphic, electronic, or mechanical, including photocopying, taping, and recording, without prior written permission from the publisher.

First US edition 2021

Library of Congress Catalog Card Number pending
ISBN 978-1-5362-1772-8

21 22 23 24 25 26 CCP 10 9 8 7 6 5 4 3 2 1

Printed in Shenzhen, Guangdong, China

This book was typeset in Nevis.
The illustrations were done in mixed media.

Candlewick Press
99 Dover Street
Somerville, Massachusetts 02144

www.candlewick.com